Righteousness
Consciousness

EMMANUEL ATOE

WESTBOW
PRESS®
A DIVISION OF THOMAS NELSON
& ZONDERVAN

WestBow Press books may be ordered through booksellers or by contacting:

WestBow Press
A Division of Thomas Nelson & Zondervan
1663 Liberty Drive
Bloomington, IN 47403
www.westbowpress.com
844-714-3454

ISBN: 979-8-3850-1536-8 (sc)
ISBN: 979-8-3850-1537-5 (e)

Library of Congress Control Number: 2023924379

Print information available on the last page.

WestBow Press rev. date: 01/11/2024

SPONSORSHIP PAGE

THIS BOOK IS SPONSORED BY

....

....

AS A GIFT TO

....

....

ON THIS DAY

....

"Each one must give as he has decided in his heart,
not reluctantly or under compulsion,
for God loves a cheerful giver."
(2 Corinthians 9:7, ESV)

Contents

Dedication

This book is dedicated to the Righteous in Christ

A special thanks go to those who love Right Living

The LORD bless you and keep you; The LORD make His face shine upon you and be gracious to you; The LORD lift His countenance upon you and give you peace, in Jesus' Name. Amen.

Always be full of joy in the Lord. I say it again - rejoice!

Introduction

GOD'S DIVINE POWER HAS GIVEN THE RIGHTEOUS ALL things that *pertain* to life and godliness. This is an awesome truth that all believers need to know and meditate upon until they have completely absorbed it, in order for it to edify and renew their minds. This truth in God's Words will change their thinking, habit, and behavior to live their God-given best life. Our purpose should be consciously living a righteous lifestyle daily. The scriptures encourage us to make the right choice because any decision you make will determine the benefits and blessings. We are those who have obtained precious faith through the righteousness of our God and Savior Jesus Christ. God desires that you decide to walk in the light of the gift of righteousness in Christ Jesus. The wise choice is to make decisions righteously before God all the years of your life.

> "Simon Peter, a bondservant, and apostle of Jesus Christ, To those who have obtained like precious faith with us by the righteousness of our God and Saviour Jesus Christ. Grace and peace be multiplied to you in the knowledge of God and Jesus our Lord, as His divine power has given to us all things that *pertain* to life and godliness, through the knowledge of Him who called us by glory and virtue, by which have been given to us exceedingly great and precious promises, that through

these you may be partakers of the divine nature, having
escaped the corruption *that is* in the world through lust."
— 2 PETER 1:1-4

The righteous person is in a deep relationship with the Father, Almighty God who is blessed forever and has blessed His children with every spiritual blessing in the heavenly *places* in Christ. God chose us in Him before the foundation of the world, that we should be holy and without blame before Him in love, having predestined us to adoption as sons by Jesus Christ to Himself, according to the good pleasure of His will, to the praise of the glory of His grace, by which He made us accepted in the beloved. [Ephesians 1:4].

This is for the righteous to walk in obedience to fulfil his [or her] obligations as part of the relationship because the Almighty God is always just and kind to his people, to fulfil His promises and obligations to them. Our God is always faithful; if we endure, we shall also reign with *Him.* If we deny *Him,* He also will deny us. If we are faithless, He is still faithful; He cannot deny Himself. [2 Timothy 2:13] Although all have fallen and yielded as slaves to sin, therefore falling short of God's glory, the sacrificial blood has made it obligatory for Him to redeem mankind. Without the shedding of blood, there can be no forgiveness of sins and God is faithful to do that through Christ. [Romans 3:23; Hebrew 9:23].

By dying, Jesus cancelled mankind's debt of sin so that the devil could no longer have any claim upon us. This happened because just as all sinned in Adam, and so became slaves to death and the devil, so all died and were raised to new life in Jesus, and so were liberated and redeemed from slavery to death and the devil. Now salvation, strength, the kingdom of our God, and the power of His Christ have come, for the accuser of our brethren, who accused them before our God day and night, has been cast down. Believers overcame the power of darkness by the blood of the Lamb and by the word of their testimony, and they did not love their lives to death. [Revelation 12:10-12] God is righteous, His redemption affects the totality of human beings, in every sphere of our lives by restoring mankind which is the object of His creation to the original condition, as He intended for mankind before the creation of the earth.

AVOID WORLDLY WISDOM

"Simon Peter, a bondservant, and apostle of Jesus Christ, To those who have obtained like precious faith with us by the righteousness of our God and Saviour Jesus Christ: Grace and peace be multiplied to you in the knowledge of God and of Jesus our Lord [2 Peter 1:1-2]. For no other foundation can anyone lay than that which is laid, which is Jesus Christ. Let no one deceive himself. If anyone among you seems to be wise in this age, let him become a fool that he may become wise. For the wisdom of this world is foolishness with God. For it is written, He catches the wise in their craftiness and again, The LORD knows the thoughts of the wise, that they are futile. Therefore let no one boast about men. For all things are yours: whether Paul or Apollos or Cephas, or the world or life or death, or things present or things to come - all are yours. And you *are* Christ's, and Christ *is* God's."

— 1 CORINTHIANS 3:11, 18-23

There is none righteous, no not one for all have sinned and fallen short of God's glory. Thanks be to God for He made Jesus who had never committed any sin to be sin for us, that we might become the righteousness of God in Him. [Romans 3:23-24] The wonderful plan of salvation is that those who put their faith in Jesus, receive life, for by grace you have been saved through faith, and that not of yourselves; *it is* the gift of God, not of works, lest anyone should boast. [Ephesians 2:8-10] The truth is by faith in Christ, you get your desire, and those who don't put their total faith in Christ will ultimately get what they deserve. The lies and deception of the adversary, have subtly taught people to trust in their goodness and holiness instead of God's mercy. This is the path of self-righteousness and eternal condemnation.

But if we walk in the light as God is in the light, we have fellowship with one another, and the blood of Jesus Christ His Son cleanses us from all sin. [1 John 1:7.9] If you're the righteous in Christ, you're clean because of the word that Jesus had spoken to you. His mighty power sanctifies and cleanses believers with the washing of water by the Word, so that He might present them to Himself a glorious church, not having spot or wrinkle or any such thing, but that you should be holy and without blemish. [Ephesian 5:27]

The righteous are to abide in our Lord Jesus Christ, and Christ in him [or her]. As the branch cannot bear fruit of itself, unless it abides in the vine, neither can the righteous, unless you abide in Jesus. Jesus is the vine; you are the branches. The righteous who abides in Jesus, and Jesus in him [or her], bears much fruit; for without Jesus, the righteous can do nothing. [John 15:4-5] God is Holy or Righteous and has commanded us to be holy and walk in Christ's righteousness.

We must depend on God's righteousness, which is a gift we receive through faith for us to live victoriously in Christ Jesus. Our righteousness falls far short of God's righteousness and no mankind can reach that through their strength. You cannot do anything to be righteous or perform well enough to obtain righteousness. No person will ever become righteous by their own abilities or capabilities because our righteousnesses are as filthy rags [Isaiah 64:4] We receive the righteousness of God in Christ Jesus by faith. [Romans 3:22] We must be conscious of Christ's righteousness, receive it by faith, walk in the light of it, and dwell in Him in complete obedience. The reality that God created mankind to live in a righteous relationship with Him is affirmed throughout the Scriptures. For in him we live, and move, and have our being; for we are also his offspring.

There is nothing to do apart from living by trust, faith, and obedience to God's Words. Any other attempt through our human effort to obtain or attain the right standing with the Lord is grossly inadequate because when we come to Jesus and we receive His salvation by faith, we are given His righteousness.

Do you not know that if you present yourselves to anyone as obedient slaves, you are slaves of the one whom you obey, either of sin, which leads to death, or of obedience, which leads to righteousness? [Romans 6:16] Jesus Christ to the righteous has become our wisdom, righteousness, sanctification, and redemption. Everyone that is born of Him, must have a conscious right mindset, i.e., the "righteousness of God in Christ Jesus" as the scripture says, "we have the mind of Christ." [1 Corinthians 2:16]. According to the scriptures "As He is, so are we in this world."

ONE

Establish In Righteousness

THE DESIRE OF EVERY BORN AGAIN SHOULD BE TO gain Christ. To strive to be found in Him, not having our righteousness, but that which *is* through faith in Christ. The righteousness which is from God by faith that we may know Jesus and the power of His resurrection, and the fellowship of His sufferings, being conformed to His death. Jesus is the son of God manifest in the flesh and was, is and will always be in a righteous relationship with God. Holy and Pure and without sin, yet He became sin for us, through no wrongdoing on His part because He bore our sins in his body on the cross, so that we might die to sins and live for righteousness.

> "But what things were gain to me, these I have counted loss for Christ. Yet indeed I also count all things loss for the excellence of the knowledge of Christ Jesus my Lord, for whom I have suffered the loss of all things, and count them as rubbish, that I may gain Christ and be found in Him, not having my righteousness, which *is* from the law, but that which *is* through faith in Christ, the righteousness which is from God by faith that I may know Him and the power of His resurrection, and the fellowship of His sufferings, being conformed to His death, if, by any means, I may attain to the resurrection from the dead."
> — PHILIPPIANS 3:7-11

1

Emmanuel Atoe

FOLLOW RIGHTEOUSNESS

Let us consciously follow righteousness and holiness because as our God which has called you is Holy, so be you holy in all manner of conversation; because it is written, 'Be ye holy; for I am holy,'. Do not allow anyone to deceive you with empty words, for because of such things God's wrath comes on those who are disobedient. [1 Peter 1:15-16; Ephesians 5:6-9]. Therefore, do not be partners with them for you were once darkness, but now you are light in the Lord, therefore live as children of light. The fruit of the light consists in all goodness, truth, and righteousness. Seek what pleases the Lord. God's desire for mankind is to be proven in this knowledge of righteousness.

God wants us to grow, so that we no longer remain children, tossed to and from and carried about with every wind of doctrine by the sleight of men and their cunning and craftiness, whereby they lie in wait to deceive. [Ephesians 4:14]. God desires that you be fully and completely established in this new covenant truth The Lord commands us to always speak the truth in love, so that we will grow to become in every respect the mature body of him who is the head, that is, Christ to be made new in the attitude of your minds; and to put on the new self, created to be like God in true righteousness and holiness.

Conscious righteousness will change your life. There is a fight of faith and the need to stand firm and to be boldly established in His righteousness. You must be fully convinced of the truth of knowing that you are right with God. Surely the righteous shall give thanks to the name of the Lord. The upright shall dwell in God's presence, but He will not let a slanderer be established on the earth, because God's righteousness is through faith in Christ Jesus. [Psalm 140:10-13]

Right from Abraham to date, we are encouraged to be established and live in conscious righteousness. Even so, Abraham believed in God, and it was reckoned to him as righteousness. But now the righteousness of God apart from the law is revealed, being witnessed by the law and

2

the prophet even the righteousness of God, through faith in Jesus Christ, to all and on all who believe. For there is no difference; for all have sinned and fallen short of the glory of God, being justified freely by His grace through the redemption that is in Christ Jesus, whom God set forth *as* a propitiation by His blood, through faith, to demonstrate His righteousness, because in His forbearance God had passed over the sins that were previously committed, to demonstrate His righteousness in this present time, that He might be just and the justifier of the one who has faith in Jesus. [Genesis 15:6; Romans 3:21-26]

We have been taken from darkness to His glorious light and recreated in the righteousness of God so that we can come boldly to the throne of grace, that we may obtain mercy and find grace to help in time of need. We are created in Christ and God's gift of righteousness is available by faith for everyone that believes. This is a gift that every believer have because of the precious, cleansing blood of Jesus. All you must do is to receive it by faith, just as Abraham believed and God granted him righteousness. [Hebrew 4:16; Romans 3:25]

> "In righteousness, you shall be established; You shall be
> far from oppression, for you shall not fear; And from
> terror, for it shall not come near you."
> — ISAIAH 54:14

This is the oath which God swore to our father Abraham: to grant us that we, being delivered from the hand of our enemies, might serve Him without fear, in holiness and righteousness before Him all the days of our life. Abraham was blessed by the Lord, not because of his works. Blessed be the God and Father of our Lord Jesus Christ, who has blessed us with every spiritual blessing in the heavenly places in Christ. You don't cry to be blessed because you are already blessed if you are born-again and established in God's righteousness. It is yours, so receive this gift by faith. [Luke 1:73-75; Ephesians 1:3-6]

We are covenant children of the Almighty God. In the Old Testament, we read about God's covenant with Abraham. His seed Jesus Christ is the Mediator of the new covenant. The work of Jesus is the establishment and perfection of the new covenant. [Hebrew 8:6, 9:15]. However, our God has revealed Himself as a covenant God - The Lord who deals faithfully with us as His family and relates directly with us individually through the Holy Spirit. We must bow down in reverence and faith, responding rightly to God's promise of a covenant relationship. It is not by might nor by power, but by My Spirit, says the LORD of hosts. [Zechariah 4:6].

THERE IS POWER WHEN WE WALK IN RIGHTEOUSNESS CONSCIOUSNESS

Our strength comes from living righteously before God and declaring His Words. This gives us entrance into the favor of God, to receive spiritual and interior strength to deal with the issues of life. Righteousness Consciousness always gives us bold entrance to the throne of the Highest. It gives us boldness, faith, and a positive result in our prayers because the effectual fervent prayer of a righteous man availed much. [James 5:16]. As the scriptures have revealed, "But it is from Him that you are in Christ Jesus, who became to us wisdom from God [revealing His plan of salvation], and righteousness [making us acceptable to God], and sanctification [making us holy and setting us apart for God], and redemption [providing our ransom from the penalty for sin]." [I Corinthians 1:30]. God has laid up for the righteous all goodliness for a blessed lifestyle. Righteousness Consciousness gives you the boldness and sound wisdom that you are acceptable to God and makes all your ways to be established. This gives you the grace to always live in His presence because you are in Christ Jesus, who has become for us, wisdom from God.

That is fullness of joy, because Christ is, our righteousness, holiness, and redemption. It empowers you to always put on the breastplate of righteousness and to guard one of the most important parts of your body. This enables you to keep your heart with all diligence, for out of it *spring* the issues of life. [Proverbs 4:23]. In the scriptures, the Almighty God commands us to protect our hearts, for everything we do flows from it. As water reflects the face, so one's life reflects the heart.

Being established in Righteousness Consciousness will make you walk in continuous communion with God through the power of the Holy Spirit. It is like the disinfectant against i.e. evil thoughts, negative imaginations, and fear that comes from the adversary's oppression and attack of terror. When you are conscious of your position as the righteousness of God, in Christ Jesus and truly rooted or established in

Christ's righteousness, you will certainly live a life of what the scriptures say in the book of Daniel "….The people who know their God shall be strong and carry out great exploits." [Daniel 11:32].

My friends, in all of your endeavors, being established in a mindset of Righteousness Consciousness will give you boldness, favor, protection, and blessing and promote you and make you victorious over those who oppose you. This can be achieved by having peace in your heart knowing you are righteous in Christ. There is holy boldness in meditating on the truth and walking in Righteousness Consciousness. As you, therefore, have received Christ Jesus the Lord, so walk in Him, rooted, built up in Him, and established in the faith, as you have been taught, abounding in it with thanksgiving. [Colossians 2:6-7].

We are in Christ Jesus and the more Righteousness Conscious we are, of His Presence, and the truth of who Jesus is, the more we are boldly established in the faith. The result is a victorious lifestyle. Jesus is "the way, the truth, and the life", [John 14:6] and only in Him, can we truly enjoy real power, safety, protection, the fullness of joy, and abundant life. "Many are the afflictions of the righteous, but the Lord delivers him out of them all" [Psalm 34:19].

TWO

Righteous By Faith

THE RIGHTEOUS SHALL LIVE BY FAITH

"Behold the proud, His soul is not upright in him; But the just shall live by his faith."

— HABAKKUK 2:4

The choices that you make in life are not without consequences. Faith is a gift from God and righteousness of God in Christ is also a gift, but it is your choice to decide to live righteously. Righteousness Consciousness is a choice. The victory that overcomes this world is our faith in Christ Jesus. For whosoever is born of God overcomes the world, and this is the victory that overcomes the world, even our faith. The truth is that you are not only victorious but more than a conqueror in Christ Jesus. Our Father and Lord, in His infinite kindness and love, has sent Jesus, so that our sin might receive its deserved condemnation, and his righteousness might receive its deserved glorification. Salvation and righteousness are the amazing grace of God. The truth of the word is that just as Abraham believed the Lord, and He reckoned it to him as righteousness, the righteousness which God requires from us comes by faith, and it is a gift. God has made this freely available by grace for all sinners because Christ died for our sins. [1 John 5:4; Romans 8:37; Genesis 15:6].

> "For therein is the righteousness of God revealed from
> faith to faith: as it is written, The just shall live by faith."
> — ROMANSNS 1:17

Those who by faith have received salvation and righteousness should walk continuously by faith enjoying the amazing grace of God. We then as workers together with the Lord Jesus by His Spirit dwelling in us, are commanded that we receive not the grace of God in vain. Conscious righteousness can describe those who act in such a way that their behavior accords with some standards. The righteous person is not sin conscious but of his position in Christ.

> But now the righteousness of God apart from the
> law is revealed, being witnessed by the Law and the
> Prophets, even the righteousness of God, through faith
> in Jesus Christ, to all and on all who believe. For there
> is no difference; for all have sinned and fall short of
> the glory of God, being justified freely by His grace
> through the redemption that is in Christ Jesus, whom
> God set forth *as* a propitiation by His blood, through
> faith, to demonstrate His righteousness, because in His
> forbearance God had passed over the sins that were
> previously committed, to demonstrate at present His
> righteousness, that He might be just and the justifier of
> the one who has faith in Jesus."
> — ROMANSNS 3:21-26

Righteousness Consciousness declares by faith that there is no condemnation to them that walk not after the flesh but after the Spirit of the living God. [Romans 8:1]. The righteousness of the law is fulfilled in everyone who dwells daily in God's presence by faith. The Spirit and life in Christ Jesus empower you to be victorious and be more than conquerors in life. This is the victory that overcomes the world, our faith in Christ Jesus because the righteous live by faith. The righteous person has a conscious faith in the atonement of a sacrificial substitute. God looks at our faith and counts us as righteous when we trust, believe the finished works of our Lord Jesus Christ, and live righteous before Him. We sinners can have that done for us because Christ took the punishment for our iniquities on himself. The scriptures say, in the book of Isaiah 53:11, "And by His knowledge, will the righteous one, my servant, make many righteous, and He shall bear their sin." There is great news for all who accept that they are sinners and God is Holy. God reckons everyone who accepts Jesus Christ as righteous because Jesus died for all mankind and because anyone who trusts in Him, is justified by faith, which is the heart of the gospel.

Faith in the finished work of Jesus is how you receive undeserved justification. There is therefore now no condemnation to those who are in Christ Jesus and having been justified by faith, we have peace with God through our Lord Jesus Christ. Blessed is the person that does not work but trusts Him and who justifies the ungodly, such a person's faith is reckoned as righteousness. [Romans 5:1].

Righteousness Consciousness is affirming by faith that God in His infinite mercy, grace, and love for the world, sent Jesus, so that our sin might receive its deserved condemnation and His righteousness might receive its deserved glorification. However, let us not forget that the scriptures admonish us that God has fixed a day on which he will judge the world in righteousness. [Acts 17:31].

"But that no man is justified by the law in the sight of God, it is evident: for, The just shall live by faith."

> "Because He has appointed a day on which He will judge the world in righteousness by the Man whom He has ordained. He has given assurance of this to all by raising Him from the dead."
> — GALATIANS 3:1; ACTS 17:31

In a time of difficulties and tribulations, those who hold firm to their faith in God will have a right to stand before man and God. A righteous person is also one who has faith in the unfailing Word of God. Faith in God is faith in His promises. God can do exceedingly abundantly above all that we ask or think, according to the power that works in us. The righteous lives by faith which please God and his [or her] heart's desire is satisfied. [Ephesians 3:20; Habakkuk 2:4].

It's important to always strive to have a righteous standing before both people and God. The righteous are those who have faith in God's grace and mercy, which provides them with security from God's wrath. The lifestyle of a righteous person consists of living daily in faith in God. The Lord is our light and salvation, meaning He delivers, protects, preserves, and provides divine health and safety.

Having faith in God and His promises that never fail is the key to securing a righteous life and eternity in safety. There is no other source of security outside of Jesus Christ. To achieve true eternal security, one must live by faith in Him every day. Jesus Christ is the only guarantee of eternal peace, safety, and security. Those who are righteous live by faith and have faith in God. Righteousness and consciousness of God in Christ Jesus come through faith, and it is available to everyone who accepts Jesus as their Lord, as the scriptures say, Christ died for our sins.

> "For I delivered to you first of all that which I also received: that Christ died for our sins according to the Scriptures, and that He was buried, and that He rose again the third day according to the Scriptures".
> — CORINTHIANS 15:3-4

The almighty Father shows His love toward us, in that while we were still sinners, Christ died for us. Righteousness Consciousness is what makes Apostle Paul through the Holy Spirit say this about himself, and it also applies to us today - the righteous in Christ. In 1 Timothy

1:15 "This is a faithful saying and worthy of all acceptance, that Christ Jesus came into the world to save sinners, of whom I am chief."

> "But God commendeth his love toward us, in that, while we were yet sinners, Christ died for us. Much more than, being now justified by his blood, we shall be saved from wrath through him. For if, when we were enemies, we were reconciled to God by the death of his Son, much more, being reconciled, we shall be saved by his life".
>
> — ROMANS 5:8-10

THREE

Righteousness Endureth Forever

IS IT TRUE THAT RIGHTEOUSNESS ENDURES FOREVER? The Lord's righteousness stands the test of time. We all cherish our wonderful past encounters, and happy memories of the past provide us with joy. We are aware that they are vulnerable to change because things in this world do not last forever. Right standing with the living God is the only thing that endures eternally. Blessed is the man who fears the Lord and who greatly delights in His commands. [Psalm 112:1].

The scriptures instruct us not to remember the past and to pay no heed to the things of the past because, as it says, "Behold, I will do a new thing, now it shall spring forth; shall you not know it? I will even make a road in the wilderness and rivers in the desert." [Isaiah 43:19]. When we realize that this world and everything in it is unstable and unpredictable, we seek something that lasts forever by faith.

Is there anything that lasts forever? What is it that lasts forever? God's faithfulness and His goodness and mercy remain forever. God's great grace has not and will not be affected by the passage of time. It cannot be taken away by anything that occurs in this life; it is everlasting. The anchor is strictly by placing our faith in the finished works of our Lord and Saviour Jesus Christ. We look with faith in our heart unto Jesus the Author and finisher of our faith. We look deeply with hope in our hearts to be able to receive help and answers to our petitions at the throne of grace.

We can approach God because we have received and believed in this conscious righteousness through Christ, who is also our life. Our salvation, our rock, and our good standing before God are found in Jesus. We can only experience true, abiding joy and permanent peace in Christ's conscious righteousness. When we take joy in the Lord and His Word, we find true contentment in life. The only way you receive eternal righteousness is through faith in Jesus Christ.

CHRIST IN OUR PLACE

"For when we were still without strength, in due time Christ died for the ungodly. For scarcely for a righteous man will one die, yet perhaps for a good man, someone would even dare to die. But God demonstrates His love toward us, in that while we were still sinners, Christ died for us."

— ROMANS 5:6-8

ENCOURAGING AND CHALLENGING YOU TO SEEK INTIMACY WITH GOD EVERY DAY

"But Abram said, Lord GOD, what will You give me, seeing I go childless, and the heir of my house *is* Eliezer of Damascus? Then Abram said, look, You have given me no offspring; indeed, one born in my house is my heir! And behold, the word of the LORD *came* to him, saying, This one shall not be your heir, but one who will come from your own body shall be your heir. Then He brought him outside and said, Look now toward heaven, and count the stars if you are able to number them. And He said to him, So shall your descendants be. And he believed in the LORD, and He accounted it to him for righteousness. Then He said to him, I *am* the LORD, who brought you out of Ur of the Chaldeans, to give you this land to inherit it".

— GENESIS 15:1-7

Abraham had faith in God, and the Lord had counted it as righteousness for him. God looks at our faith and counts us righteous, therefore there is a connection between believing God and being in His presence and living in His good favor. God can accomplish that for us sinners because Christ took the penalty for our transgressions upon himself. This is righteousness consciousness living in the grace of God by faith and anointing.

The stronger our faith, the greater our faith in God's intimate knowledge of this glorious inheritance in God who raised Jesus from the dead for our justification. We are the born-again children of God, recreated in Christ to live by grace every day in the anointing of the Holy Spirit, as righteousness-conscious, living saints in Christ Jesus.

"Yet it pleased the LORD to bruise him; he hath put him to grief: when thou shalt make his soul an offering for sin, he shall see his seed, he shall prolong his days, and the pleasure of the LORD shall prosper in his hand. He shall see of the travail of his soul and shall be satisfied: by his knowledge shall my righteous servant justify many; for he shall bear their iniquities."

— ISAIAH 53:10-11

The heart of the gospel, the best news in the world to those who know they are sinners and God is Holy, is when God counts a person righteous because Christ died for him and because he places his trust in Christ. This is what we call justification by faith. Every believer should grow and live by faith in a righteousness consciousness lifestyle.

"Now the just shall live by faith: but if any man draws back, my soul shall have no pleasure in him."

— HEBREWS 10:38

Righteousness Consciousness is believing in God and enjoying His favor because God judges us according to the strength of our faith and counts us as virtuous. It is because Christ took the punishment for our trespasses upon himself that God can achieve that for us sinners. The scriptures clearly states in Isaiah 53:11: "By his knowledge the righteous one, my servant, shall cause many to be declared righteous; and he shall bear their iniquities." We refer to this as justification by faith and it is the core of the gospel.

"Take delight in the LORD, and he will give you the desires of your heart. But now the righteousness of God apart from the law is revealed, being witnessed by the Law and the Prophets, even the righteousness of God, through faith in Jesus Christ, to all and on all who believe. For there is no difference; for all have sinned and fallen short of the glory of God, being justified freely by His grace through the redemption that is in Christ Jesus, whom God set forth *as* a propitiation by His

blood, through faith, to demonstrate His righteousness, because in His forbearance God had passed over the sins that were previously committed, to demonstrate at the present time His righteousness, that He might be just and the justifier of the one who has faith in Jesus."
— ROMANS 3:21-26

Everyone who recognizes their sinfulness, and the Holiness of God knows that when God counts someone as righteous, you are righteous. Righteousness consciousness is affirming boldly that Christ died for him [or her]and the individual places his [or her] faith in Christ. It does not depend on what others think or doesn't think about you, what matters is your faith in the word of God.

There may be more here than we think for the encouragement of our faith. The judgment of God is coming to those who walk and live in self-righteousness unless they repent. Our righteousness is Christ and if you're living a holy and righteous life in Christ, His righteousness will exalt you. It will give you the peace of God which no one can ever give or take away from you.

"But that no man is justified by the law in the sight of God, it is evident: for, The just shall live by faith."
— GALATIANS 3:1

God Almighty has made it possible by giving us the invitation of love to come boldly to the throne of grace so that we may gain mercy and find grace to help in times of need. [Hebrews 4:16]. A prominent man of God in the early American church defines God's righteousness as "the ability to stand in the presence of the Father God without a sense of guilt or inferiority." God wants the righteous to walk in bold faith in the finished work of our Lord Jesus.

"The wicked flee when no one pursues them, but the righteous are bold as a lion."
— PROVERBS 28:1

Righteousness consciousness affirms strongly that the moment you accept the Lord Jesus as your Lord and Saviour, God becomes your righteousness. This means you come into a "royal family" and "royal state". Those born again in Christ Jesus are accepted by God to rule as kings or queens in this world. They are formed in the image and likeness of Almighty God.

> "What is man that you remember him, or a son of man whom you love? You made him a little lower than the angels. You have crowned him with glory and honour. You made him ruler over them You have made him ruler over the works of your hands; You put everything under his feet."
>
> — PSALM 8:4-6

Kings and queens are bold and cannot live in condemnation. The devil is an expert at judgment and uses our mistakes and shortcomings as an opportunity to bring about judgment, a sense of guilt, and disapproval. Condemnation forces people to run from God, fellowship, and communities of life because they wrongly think their weaknesses are unique. The adversary like to use this weakness because he wants us to isolate ourselves and maybe try to avoid God. There are a lot of consequences that might come with this false and trap intervention. Our right standing before God cannot be overturned. The Bible tells us that Jesus Christ is our Advocate"

> "My little children, these things I write to you, so that you may not sin. And if anyone sins, we have an Advocate with the Father, Jesus Christ the righteous."
>
> — 1 JOHN 2:1

THE TEST OF KNOWING CHRIST

The accuser of the brethren, often known as the devil, works overtime to convince Christians to accept his accusations. He accuses us of being guilty, wrong, and ashamed. These charges of the devil are untrue. Jesus made up for our failings and guilt. Nobody should be afraid of the power of darkness, particularly those walking in the light of God's Righteousness consciousness. Jesus' death on the cross was a significant transaction.

We were made righteous by His righteousness, and He became sin through our transgression against divine law. The truth is that Jesus gave us a perfect standing before God despite all of our flaws. Nothing can keep us apart from God's mercy and love. The prince of darkness according to the scriptures is the accuser of our brethren who knows how to disseminate condemnation - a sense of guilt and disapproval. The power of darkness takes advantage of our failings and errors.

People who feel condemned are compelled to flee from God, the place of worship, and fellow believers because they incorrectly think their flaws are particular to them. In most cases, they are deceived by the lies of the devil – the "father of all lies". [John 8:44]. Through deception these individuals fall further into the trap of the enemy by isolating themselves and, in certain cases, attempting to get rid of God and all the repercussions of His intervention.

> "And the great dragon was cast out, that old serpent, called the Devil, and Satan, which deceiveth the whole world: he was cast out into the earth, and his angels were cast out with him. And I heard a loud voice saying in heaven, Now is come salvation and strength, and the kingdom of our God, and the power of his Christ: for the accuser of our brethren is cast down, which accused them before our God day and night. And they overcame him by the blood of the Lamb, and by the

word of their testimony, and they loved not their lives
unto the death."

— REVELATION 12:9-11

Christians are the target of Satan, the accuser of the brethren, to
bring his accusations and condemnations. He charges the mind with
greater guilt, condemnation, humiliation, shame, and fear than the
actual failure or situation. The charges of the devil are untrue because
of Lord Jesus' ferocious atonement for our failings. Nobody should be
afraid of the forces of darkness, including persecutors.

There was a unique interchange that happened when Jesus died on
the cross. He became sin through our transgression, and through His
righteousness, we are made right or justified by God. Jesus said the devil
was a murderer from the beginning and does not stand in the truth,
because there is no truth in him. When he speaks a lie, he speaks from
his own *resources,* for he is a liar and the father of it. [John 8:44].

Righteous Declaration

MY TONGUE SHALL SPEAK OF THE RIGHTEOUSNESS of God every day of my life. As the scriptures say in Psalm 35:27, "Let them shout for joy, and be glad, that favour my righteous cause, yes, let them say continually, let the LORD be magnified, which hath pleasure in the prosperity of his servant." The believer who wants to be victorious in Christ Jesus should have his [her] heart filled with gladness and full of joy, which comes forth in a tongue that speaks of God's righteousness *and* praise.

> "My mouth shall tell of Your righteousness *And* Your salvation all the day, For I do not know *their* limits. I will go in the strength of the Lord GOD; I will make mention of Your righteousness, of Yours only."
> — PSALMS 71:15-16

God is love; therefore transgression nature of sinful man and the consequent guilty verdict cannot hinder the love of God and the grace of the free gift of righteousness. All of us have sinned and because of our transgression, we have come short of the glory of God. Everyone born of a woman is guilty in the presence of God. We come short of the glory of God and have an absolute need for His mercy and grace. Once we have been saved, our body of sin is buried with Christ, and we are raised up as new creatures who now have new natures: These natures are free to submit to obedience by the power of the Holy Spirit. In His grace and perfect love, God has declared everyone who has accepted Jesus Christ as their Savior and washed in the blood, not guilty, acquitted, and justified. This verdict from the throne of grace brings them into the perfect righteousness of God.

That is the righteousness of God which is by the faith of Jesus Christ upon everyone that believes. As the scriptures say, "For if by the one man's offense death reigned through the one, much more those who receive abundance of grace and of the gift of righteousness will reign in life through the One, Jesus Christ." [Romans 5:17]. The free gift of righteousness that Almighty God, in His infinite and wonderful love and grace, has given to all who believe in the sacrificial death of Jesus Christ on the cross Calvary.

> "And my tongue shall speak of Your righteousness *And*
> of Your praise all the day long."
> — PSALMS 35:28

Praise is a sign of gratitude in the mouth of those who are called to reign. Every believer by faith receives the abundance of Grace in our daily walk with God, so that we can reign in life. The love of God gave Jesus as a gift for our salvation and righteousness because no individual can save themselves from eternal damnation by his [or her] effort or power. How much more will those who receive God's abundant provision of grace and the gift of righteousness reign in life through the one man, Jesus Christ?

God's undeserved favor on His cherished family, which comes by faith that it might be by Grace. The Just shall live by faith which derives from hearing and hearing the word of God. When we listen and study the Word of God, we build our faith until we begin to become established in Jesus' righteousness.

God remembers His holy covenant, the oath which He swore to our Father Abraham to grant us that we, being delivered from the hand of our enemies, might serve Him without fear, in holiness and righteousness before Him all the days of our life. Righteousness consciousness is that we shall be free of fear and oppression of the enemy.

ZACHARIAH PROPHECY

"Now his father Zacharias was filled with the Holy Spirit, and prophesied, saying: Blessed *is* the Lord God of Israel, For He has visited and redeemed His people, And has raised up a horn of salvation for us In the house of His servant David, As He spoke by the mouth of His holy prophets, Who *have been* since the world began, That we should be saved from our enemies And from the hand of all who hate us, To perform the mercy *promised* to our fathers And to remember His holy covenant, The oath which He swore to our father Abraham: To grant us that we, being delivered from the hand of our enemies, might serve Him without fear, In holiness and righteousness before Him all the days of our life. And you, child, will be called the prophet of the Highest; For you will go before the face of the Lord to prepare His ways, To give knowledge of salvation to His people By the remission of their sins, Through the tender mercy of our God, With which the Dayspring from on high has visited us; To give light to those who sit in darkness and the shadow of death, To guide our feet into the way of peace. So, the child grew and became strong in spirit, and was in the deserts till the day of his manifestation to Israel."

— LUKE 1:67-80

As we continue to feed on God's Word, and make declarations with our mouths, we grow spiritually in grace from receiving God's undeserved favor. The scriptures say, in 2 Corinthians 4:13. "Since we have that same spirit of faith, we also believe and therefore speak." Our tongues shall speak of Your word, for all Your commandments are righteousness. Throughout our Christian life, we are called to feed on and confess the bread of life. This is a continuous process and not only something you heard in the past. It is the process of continuous hearing and declaration of God's Word that brings the faith needed to be established in our hearts and to live the powerful gift of Jesus' Righteousness.

This gives you the power to boldly reign in life daily declaring, without doubt, or fear what faith is building in your heart. A righteousness consciousness declaration is a holy and bold proclamation of faith from the heart because the mouth confesses, and demons of fear and oppression have no choice but to flee as the heart believes the Word of faith. A confirmation of the scriptures in 2 Corinthians 4:13, "I believed; therefore, I have spoken."

> "My Tongue also shall talk of Your righteousness all the day long; For they are confounded, For they are brought to shame Who seek my hurt."
> — PSALMS 71:24

A Christian who lives in righteousness consciousness is bold because the wicked flee when no one pursues, but the righteous are as bold as a lion: [Proverbs 28:1]. We have nothing to fear but to reign in life with an abundance of God's Grace and the Gift of Righteousness. The righteous person makes bold declarations, because the just shall live by faith, and oppression of the forces of darkness cannot continue in the life of whosoever is born again and established in Righteousness. He or [she] must believe and receive favor by faith. Righteousness is your gift of God's Grace or undeserved favor, so receive it with thanks and praises by faith.

Righteousness Consciousness is a life of continuous bold declarations of God's grace and not by our right actions. God has given His grace to every believer freely so that we can reign in life by Jesus. The scriptures say, "Let them shout for joy and be glad, who favor my righteous cause; and let them say continually, let the Lord be magnified, who has pleasure in the prosperity of His servant." [Psalm 35:27]. Our tongue should always speak of God's righteousness and His praise should be in our mouths every day. We are to hope continually and keep praising the Lord more and more, in our lives. We are to talk about His righteousness and salvation every day of our lives.

FIVE

Righteous Holy Boldness

"The wicked flee when no one pursues, But the righteous are bold as a lion. Because of the transgression of a land, many *are* its princes; But by a man of understanding *and* knowledge Right will be prolonged."
— PROVERBS 28:1-2

Righteous consciousness is the power to be bold and have a life full of joy and gladness even in case of difficulties. The desire of mankind is happiness in life and a craving for security and safety which is a common factor throughout all races and generations of time. The Lord never promises you won't have challenges or trials in life. The scripture says, "Many are the afflictions of the righteous, but the Lord delivers him out of them all." [Psalm 34:19] The forces of darkness will give the righteous trouble in the world but victory comes from faith in God.

"He who sins is of the devil, for the devil has sinned from the beginning. For this purpose, the Son of God was manifested, that He might destroy the works of the devil."
— 1 JOHN 3:8-9

The prince of the air or the god of this world will do his best to persecute and put pressure on you to disobey God. Satan will tempt you to reject the authority of God and become like God or walk in self-righteousness. The strategy of the forces of darkness is to nurture and cultivate the pride that puts selfishness or desires above the law of God. This is self-righteousness, lawlessness, pride, and disobedience to God.

This is the root cause or nature of sin; and the main reason Jesus was manifested to destroy the works of the devil in mankind. In His ministry on earth, the Lord Jesus destroyed the works of the devil. Christ as the Son of God was manifested so that He might undo and destroy the sinful deeds of the devil, that is, condemn the sin started by him! [1 John 3:8].

The Lord has promised to deliver the righteous out of all troubles, so whatever the challenges or trials God is our ever-present help to save and deliver us. This is the joy of those whose hope and help are in the Lord.

> "Praise the LORD, O my soul! While I live, I will praise the LORD; I will sing praises to my God while I have my being. Do not put your trust in princes, *Nor* in a son of man, in whom *there is* no help. His spirit departs, and he returns to his earth; In that very day, his plans perish. Happy *is he* who *has* the God of Jacob for his help, whose hope *is* in the LORD his God, Who made heaven and earth, The sea, and all that *is* in them; Who keeps truth forever, Who executes justice for the oppressed, Who gives food to the hungry. The LORD gives freedom to the prisoners. The LORD opens *the eyes of* the blind; The LORD raises those who are bowed down; The LORD loves the righteous."
>
> — PSALM 146:1-8

THE LORD LOVES THE RIGHTEOUS

The righteous God loves those who are the righteousness of God in Christ Jesus. If we know that He is righteous, we know that everyone that doeth righteousness is born of Him. [1 John 2:29]. We should boldly make great efforts to understand God's laws and be diligent to be obedient to His commandments. Our righteousness is in Christ, but we must play our part to walk in the light of His righteousness and thus be worthy of the promised protection and blessings.

There is great joy and happiness in striving to live a bold righteous life. The plan of God for His children is that they live in obedience to His laws. We cannot live in immorality and disobedience to God's commandments without reaping the consequence of such actions. Disobedience to the laws of God is denying His authority and acceptance of the things that are wrong. God is Holy therefore righteous holy boldness is the core of all the attributes of God. A Godlike attribute for any person who is righteous and walk in the righteousness of God in Christ Jesus.

"Blessed *are* those who keep justice, *And* he who does righteousness at all times!"

— PSALM 106:3

Righteous holy boldness is a life commitment for all that is good and holy. It includes the principles of power and the heavenly law by which all of God's things are handled, controlled, and managed. Let no one deceive you because anyone that does righteousness is righteous, even as God is righteous. Therefore, being justified by faith, we have peace with God through our Lord Jesus. [Romans 5:1].

In righteousness there is the fulfillment of faith and hope. Every blessing God has promised His children is based on obedience to His Laws and commandments. There are a lot of life challenges and trials related to family, business, work, oppression, loneliness, persecution, abuse, poverty, rejection, health, security, and an endless list but thanks be to God in Christ Jesus there is hope and the solution to all these challenges is faith in God and bold righteousness. In righteousness, there is safety and security but if you suffer for righteousness' sake, happy [are you] and be not afraid of their terror, neither be troubled.

The God of all grace, who has called us unto His eternal glory by Christ Jesus, after that you have suffered a while, make you perfect, establish, strengthen, settle [you]. [1 Peter 5:10]. However, Whosoever committed sin also transgressed the law: for sin is the transgression of the law. Repentance leads to righteousness because where there is disobedience to the law and commandments of God, there is repentance. If we confess our sins, instead of affirming our self-righteousness, God is faithful and just to forgive us and cleanse us from every form of unrighteousness. [1John 1:9].

We should in humility and brokenness confess our sins because the Lord will be faithful to his promise of mercy, and just in requiring us to have the atonement of Christ. The only one who could offer such a sacrifice is Jesus Christ. Since He was immaculate, He was not subject to spiritual death and because He is the Only Begotten Son of an immortal God, He had power over physical death. The gift of immortality, which will be received by all, and the gift of eternal life, which can only be accessed through the condition of repentance, were brought about by Jesus Christ's Atonement with His unique birthright to forgive us our sins. However, the righteous are commanded by God to flee also youthful lusts: but follow righteousness, faith, charity, and peace, with them that call on the Lord out of a pure heart. [2 Timothy 2:22]

The antithesis of righteousness is sin. The natural man is a sinner, and the scriptures say there is none righteous, not even one, and sin is lawlessness. Sin reigns in the natural man and it manifests in his relationship with others. The natural man does not understand the reason why he has nothing to do with his own righteousness, so he rejects that free gift in favor of what he considers are the good deeds he has done worthy of salvation and righteousness.

Sinners can't practice righteousness and they do not have right standing before God. The wrath of God is revealed against their ungodliness and unrighteousness. The righteousness of God, which is in Christ Jesus, is credited to those "in Christ," by imputation. This is a gift of God and no one who is justified before God has any merit of his own. Sin nature does what sin dictates and it is an enemy of righteousness.

Righteousness Consciousness is living a life of holy boldness and doing what Christ dictates because He is the Lord of our righteousness. Repentance is the pathway to righteousness because where there is disobedience to God's laws and commandments, there is repentance.

SIX

Righteous Protection And Safety

THERE IS SECRET POWER HIDDEN IN EVERY word of the Almighty God. In life, there are troubles and trials. The desires of everyone include divine health, prosperity, happiness, protection, and safety. God has granted to us everything pertaining to life. We can be assured by knowing the promises of God that there is nothing that we need that God has not supplied or will not provide for us.

We simply need to take advantage of what God has freely given us. Salvation and righteousness in God are by grace and faith. For by grace, you have been saved through faith; and that not of yourselves, it is the gift of God; not because of works, so that no one may boast. God has given all believers the measure of faith to believe that they are indeed righteous in Christ and that this righteousness is of the Lord's doing, not your own doing. [Ephesians 2:8-9; Romans 12:3]. This is how no weapon formed against you shall prosper. This is how you live an overcoming and victorious life.

> "His Divine power has given to us all things that pertain
> to life and godliness, through the knowledge of Him
> who called us by glory and virtue."
>
> — 2 PETER 1:3-4

This is the righteous protection and safety in the Lord. The great secret to unleashing the various promises of protection and safety. God has given us everything pertaining to life. We are the righteousness of God in Christ Jesus. This is your right standing. Take advantage of daily walking fully in your inheritance in Christ acknowledging that every tongue which rises against you in judgment you shall condemn.

This is the heritage of the children of the Lord and our right standing is from the almighty Lord. It is the knowledge of your righteousness which is from the Lord and your bold declaration by faith that ensures that no weapon formed against you will prosper, and every tongue of condemnation, accusation, and judgment that rises against you will fail woefully.

> "No weapon formed against you shall prosper, and
> every tongue which rises against you in judgment you
> shall condemn. This is the heritage of the servants of
> the Lord, and their righteousness is from Me," says the
> Lord."
>
> — ISAIAH 54:17

The Lord is the Lord of deliverance and all through the scriptures God in His infinite mercy delivers the righteous from trouble. The Lord intervened in the situation of Noah and Lot and saved them from a desperate situation. Both of them lived during an evil period when their respective peer groups lived in disobedience to God's plan for humanity Noah and Lot were redeemed in diverse ways. It is an example of a situation in which God intervened in perfect time and form. God knows how to deliver the righteous.

"The Lord knows how to deliver the Godly out of temptations, and to reserve the unjust unto the Day of Judgment to be punished"
— 2 PETER 2:7-9

Everyone who is born again has been declared righteous because of our relationship with Jesus Christ. As believers, we should remind ourselves continuously through daily meditation that we are declared righteous which means right standing with God the Father because of what Jesus did on the cross for us. It is pleasing to God to meditate on His Word and declare that you are a son, anointed and seated in Him. Righteousness consciousness is not focused on our sins but on what Jesus' Righteousness produces through our lives.

We need to meditate on verses that give us confidence and security. God knows how to deliver the righteous from temptations and other obstacles that work to hinder us from being secure and effective in our Christian walk

"The righteous is delivered from trouble, And it comes to the wicked instead."
— PROVERBS 11:8

God wants you to use your faith to believe that even when you are facing trials and challenges in life, He is your protection and safety. Be strong and of good courage, do not fear nor be afraid of the adversaries; for the Lord your God is always with you. He is the One who goes with you. He will not leave you nor forsake you.

God is always with us and when we fail and sin against Him instead of affirming in disobedience that we are sinless we should in humility confess our sins. If we confess our sins the Lord is "faithful" to his promise of mercy, and "just" in allowing us to have the atonement of Christ, "to forgive us our sins" The Lord God is full of love, mercy, and grace. A God who justifies the ungodly and makes them righteous.

When the "accuser of our brethren", according to Revelation 12:10, the devil comes against you and infests your thought and mind with accusatory words of condemnation about your faults, lost protection, unsafety, and lies about your Christian life, remember to always stand strong in the Lord.

Do not listen to the lies of the Devil that God will not hear your prayer. Repent from your sin. Let the sinners forsake his [or her] sin. Instead of affirming in disobedience that you are sinless you should confess your sins in humility and shut the mouth of the accuser. The moment of a crisis or challenge is the time to double up your declaration of your righteousness

In Christ Jesus, no weapon formed against you shall prosper. The accuser wants you to focus on your self-righteousness. Faith is made void and the promise made of no effect, but you should set up your mind on the things that are above - your inheritance in Christ.

Let us acknowledge God's awesome power, faithfulness, grace, and mercy declaring boldly His character and making it active in our lives. Any person who has the desire to receive divine influence that transforms the individual and impacts the world for God must walk in the light of the truth of the power of God's Righteousness consciousness, Therefore, do not throw away your confidence; it will have great recompense. [Hebrew 10:35].

Righteousness elevates us to a place where we are no longer trying to be but are convinced that we already are the children and the righteousness of God in Christ Jesus. This is the place where life is according to the will of God in our lives. Do not walk in unbelief and do not stop declaring that you are righteous in Christ, because the promises of protection and safety belong to you being a joint heir with Christ Jesus. The unmerited favor of God is your righteous inheritance. You are the righteousness of God in Christ Jesus, and the Lord will continue to fulfill His promises in every area of your life.

SEVEN

Righteous Dominion And Power

DOMINION AND POWER IS GIVEN TO THE RIGHTEOUS by the Creator. God intended for humans to reflect and resemble him. God directly created us to be His earthly ambassadors and to rule over the rest of creation in His name. Man has authority over the creations that God has created.

> "Then God said, Let Us make man in Our image, according to Our likeness; let them have dominion over the fish of the sea, over the birds of the air, and over the cattle, over all the earth and over every creeping thing that creeps on the earth."
> — GENESIS 1:26

Then God blessed them, and God said to them, be fruitful and multiply; fill the earth and subdue it and have dominion. Then sin came and man lost His dominion over Satan. In the fall of the man, Adam lost his dominion and became a slave to sin and Satan. Therefore, just as through Adam sin entered the world, and death through sin, and thus death spread to all men because all sinned.

"Moreover, the law entered that the offense might abound. But where sin abounded, grace abounded much more, so that as sin reigned in death, even so grace might reign through righteousness to eternal life through Jesus Christ our Lord."

— ROMANS 5:15-19

AUTHORITY AND POWER

Through the supernatural work of the Holy Spirit, Mary a virgin, gave birth to the Son of God. Behold, the virgin shall be with child, and bear a Son, and they shall call His name Immanuel, which is translated, as "God with us." The Son of God became a man and entered our world to bring salvation restoration power, and dominion to our lost humanity. God was well pleased with all His creation, and Jesus restored mankind to that original state.

"But the free gift *is* not like the offense. For if by the one man's offense, many died, much more the grace of God and the gift by the grace of the one Man, Jesus Christ, abounded to many. And the gift *is* not like *that which came* through the one who sinned. For the judgment *which came* from one *offense resulted* in condemnation, but the free gift *which came* from many offenses *resulted* in justification. For if by the one man's offence death reigned through the one, much more those who receive abundance of grace and of the gift of righteousness will reign in life through the One, Jesus Christ.

Therefore, through one man's offence *judgment came* to all men, resulting in condemnation, even so through one Man's righteous act *the free gift came* to all men, resulting in justification of life. For as by one man's disobedience many were made sinners, so also by one Man's obedience, many will be made righteous. Moreover, the law entered that the offense might abound. But where sin abounded, grace abounded much more, so that as sin reigned in death, even so, grace might reign through righteousness to eternal life through Jesus Christ our Lord."

— ROMANS 5:15-21

The righteous must have a clear knowledge of God's wonderful grace and mercy. The truth that we are presented by grace before God through Jesus Christ should be confidently secured in the minds of every Christian. The Amazon love of our Lord Jesus the Righteous has been demonstrated to His children, making us righteous with His Righteousness. My friends, what great love the Father has lavished on us, that we should be called children of God! And that is what we are! The reason the world does not know us is that they did not know it, because they don't know God.

> "What is man that You are mindful of him, And the son of man that You visit him? For You have made him a little lower than the angels, And You have crowned him with glory and honour. You have made him to have dominion over the works of Your hands; You have put all *things* under his feet."
> — PSALM 8:6-8

This lack of understanding of your righteousness in Christ could hinder your spiritual walk with God. This is dangerous because it produces fear and insecurity. It is the root cause of self-righteousness, operating in your own willpower, strength, and ability, and not depending on the guidance of the Holy Spirit.

> "And Jesus came and spoke to them saying, All authority has been given to Me in heaven and on earth. Go therefore and make disciples of all the nations, baptizing them in the name of the Father and of the Son and of the Holy Spirit, teaching them to observe all things that I have commanded you; and lo, I am with you always, *even* to the end of the age. Amen."
> — MATTHEW 28:18-20

Believers should grow strongly in trusting in the *Lord* with all their hearts, and not lean on their understanding. In all their ways acknowledge that God is their source, strength, and helper, who directs their paths. Insecurity restricts you from the things of God because you feel inadequate, abandoned, helpless, unprotected, and most especially unsafe. When you know that you have been made right with God, that comes through the revelation of righteousness the result is boldness. This new life in Christ is about the immortal life of God inside of us producing constant change, producing heaven on earth, and glorifying God. Be convinced that you are the righteousness of God in Christ Jesus.

The agenda of the forces of darkness is to stop believers from looking unto Jesus, the author and finisher of our faith, who for the joy that was set before Him endured the cross, despising the shame, and has sat down at the right hand of the throne of God. [Hebrews 12:2]. Human beings are deeply flawed and fallible and seek inspiration from those righteous sources. We are encouraged to fight the fight of faith by positioning ourselves to line up with God's will for reconciliation.

Although, in all these things we are more than conquerors through the Lord who loved us. [Romanas 8:37]. Insecurity restricts you from having faith in the things of God because you wrongly feel that you are not a conqueror, but a weakling. The self-righteous person is a double-minded individual who is unstable in all his ways and doomed to failure.

> "Behold, I give you the authority to trample on serpents
> and scorpions, and over all the power of the enemy, and
> nothing shall by any means hurt you.
> — LUKE 10:19

The righteous person has a mind set on things above, and does not conform to this world, but is transformed by the renewing of his [or her] mind, to prove all that is the good, acceptable, and perfect will of God. [Romans 12:2]. The nature of God is to look beyond the natural and believe in the supernatural power of God. It is self-righteous to attempt to fulfill God's Word in your strength. The strive for perfection comes from having intimacy with the Holy Spirit and is the result of righteousness consciousness.

My friends, this is the confidence that the righteous have in God, that if we ask anything according to His will, He hears us, and when we know God hears us, whatever we ask, we know that we have what we ask of Him. [1 John 5:14]. True liberty is that righteousness consciousness enables us to remain pure by yielding to the Holy Spirit. It is a good humility to put on the inheritance that God has provided for us through His Son, which enables us to attract His grace and blessings. God's Grace comes to the humble, and God's grace is the pathway to righteousness consciousness.

The Lord intends mankind's dominion by grace to be a righteous dominion, meaning one that is guided, directed, and enlightened by the Holy Spirit and the Word of God. Dominion of power, and authority by God's love for believers and our love for Him and His wonderful works. Our Lord Jesus is the perfect representation of the Father, who had mercy on sinners and forgave their sins. Jesus with love for mankind and the power of the Holy Spirit of God was upon Him and when Satan came to tempt Him, Jesus unsheathed the Word of God and ran Satan through with the sword. Jesus defeated Satan with the Holy Spirit and the Holy Scriptures; the two weapons given to man by God. The scriptures say, in Luke 10:17-18 "Then the seventy returned with joy, saying, Lord, even the demons are subject to us in Your name. and He said to them, I saw Satan fall like lightning from heaven."

> "The Lord knows how to deliver the Godly out of temptations, and to reserve the unjust unto the Day of Judgment to be punished"
>
> — 2 PETER 2:7-9

The will of God for His creation is to be able to walk in the spirit of love and forgiveness that produces right standing with God. The secret of our security and protection is walking in agreement with God. Righteousness is having our eyes set always on the finished work of Jesus and taking our eyes off our performance.

We grow in faith knowing our righteousness in Christ does not change. We are continually being transformed by the goodness of God that lives on the inside, moving us closer to the image of Christ Jesus that we have been predestined to be conformed to, according to the scriptures. Righteousness consciousness' is having no desire for sin. There is no sin conscious on the pathway of the righteous person because he [or she] who follows righteousness and mercy, finds life, righteousness, and honor.

EIGHT

Righteous Blessings And Favor

THE RIGHTEOUS IS BLESSED AND HIGHLY FAVORED.
Righteousness is the condition of being in the right relationship with
the Lord. We receive our righteousness through belief in Jesus Christ,
made possible by His perfect life, death, and resurrection on the cross.
This is an act of faith and complete dependence upon Christ.

Righteousness is a gift that comes from God to those who accept
what Jesus Christ has done for mankind by faith. Through the precious
blood of Jesus, we have legal approval for our moral status. We are not
held accountable for the debt of sin that we legally owe. Instead, it is
through Jesus that we have life and life more abundantly.

> "For it is by grace you have been saved through faith,
> and this not from yourselves; it is the gift of God."
> — EPHESIANS 2:8

Let us shout with joy and tell the righteous it will be well with
them, for they will enjoy the good fruit of their deeds. The fruit of
righteousness is a tree of life, that comes through Jesus Christ - to the
glory and praise of God. This is the fruit of your salvation, the righteous

character produced in your life by Jesus Christ. The fruit displayed in our lives comes from God and is not for our praise and glory and not to gain vain glory and self-righteousness from men; it is to glorify God, Who is the evidence of true salvation and abundant spiritual life in us. He who pursues righteousness and faithful love finds life, prosperity, and honor.

Your right standing and declaration should be I am the righteousness of God in Christ Jesus and God's love is in me. That is my identity in Christ, and I know who I am in Christ. God has made me righteous and holy in Christ so that I'll live in righteousness consciousness. The love of God is in me so that I can demonstrate compassion and kindness out of the overflow of God's favor and grace that is abundant in my life. "For everyone to whom much is given, from him much will be required; and to whom much has been committed, of him they will ask the more." [Luke 12:48]. My righteous responsibilities include making proper use of my God-given talents, abilities, gifts, and natural skills to bless other people.

Every perfect gift we receive is from above, coming down from the Father of the heavenly lights, who does not change like shifting shadows. [James 1:17]. God is the giver of life and anything good. Everything awesome that we have is a gift from God, undeserved. God expects us to use these talents to advance His kingdom regardless of how much or how little we have received. God's blessing is on the righteous; making him [or her] successful, so that he [or she] will be a blessing to mankind.

Righteousness consciousness is allowing the glory and excellency of God's goodness, and right standing to shine through us. It is allowing God's inward peace and prosperity to flow from our hearts to bring that love, compassion, and peace where it is needed. The fruit of righteousness is sown in peace by those who make peace. [James 3:18]. There is a divine substitution which is receiving graciously what we do not deserve because righteousness brings us to sonship.

We are given what the righteousness of Christ Jesus deserves. This is the wonderful grace of God that our Lord Jesus did everything right for us to have an abundant life. We enjoy God's undeserved, unearned, and unmerited favor. It is received by grace because God's divine power has given to us all things that pertain to life and godliness.

> "As His divine power has given to us all things that *pertain* to life and godliness, through the knowledge of Him who called us by glory and virtue, by which have been given to us exceedingly great and precious promises, that through these you may be partakers of the divine nature, having escaped the corruption *that is* in the world through lust."
>
> — 2 PETER 1:3-4

Righteous blessing and favor are by faith in God. Faith is the avenue by which we come to God and trust Him for our salvation. Which includes Protection, Safety, Prosperity, Devine Health, Soundness and Complete Wholeness. This aspect of faith trusts in the character of God as a Father of goodness, gracious, generosity, kindness, compassion, mercy, and full of love. God is love, and in His infinite goodness, God provides every good thing that pertains to life.

However, without faith, it is impossible to please Him, for he who comes to God must believe that He is and that He is a rewarder of those who diligently seek Him. [Hebrews 11:6]. Righteousness consciousness is living every day by faith because "the just shall live by faith." [Romans 1:17; Galatians 3:11; Hebrews 10:38]. The righteous person must have a continuous desire to draw near to God and must have a deep-rooted belief that God is real and will reward those who diligently seek Him in obedience to the faith.

An unwavering faith is found in the heart of those who are daily walking, living in His presence, and dining at His table. They praise and worship the Lord in truth and spirit. Righteousness consciousness is a truly genuine conviction that God exists, and the greatest joy is in the possibility of having an intimate relationship with Him. The result is that He rewards those who earnestly seek Him.

God knows about our imperfections, challenges, failures, and desires and we have faith and must trust Him in all situations. Righteousness consciousness is walking in the grace and faithfulness of God, acknowledging faith in His unmerited favor instead of false self-righteousness. The righteous person does not have any trust in the flesh. Our faith is not based on a selfish perfect performance, but our trust is in God who justifies the righteous declaring us blameless and putting us in a right relationship with Himself.

Therefore, righteousness consciousness is having trust. It is an unwavering faith in the Word of God and the power of the Holy Spirit that you are indeed righteous by Christ's Righteousness. There is nothing that can separate you from the love of God so that you will reign in this life as a world overcomer. We are co-heirs with the Son of the living God. Just as Abram believed the Lord and the Lord counted him as righteous because of his faith, so everyone who accepts Jesus Christ as their Lord and Savior is declared righteous by God.

Righteous consciousness is having a living faith and walking in the light that God is no longer "imputing your trespasses" to you because, through the death, burial, resurrection, and ascension of our Lord Jesus, He has settled the account of the whole world's sins forever. True believers have this knowledge that God has already made them righteous with the "Righteousness of Jesus" and clothed them with the robe of right living.

> "I will greatly rejoice in the LORD, my soul shall be joyful in my God; For He has clothed me with the garments **of** salvation, He has covered me with the robe of righteousness, As a bridegroom decks *himself*

with ornaments, And as a bride adorns *herself* with her jewels."

— ISAIAH 61:10

Jesus is our High Priest, so let us, therefore, approach God's throne of grace with confidence, so that we may receive mercy and find grace to help us in our time of need. This is not timidity but righteousness consciousness and confidence. We go boldly to the throne of grace when we have the revelation that God is not imputing our trespasses to us and has committed to us the word of reconciliation.

The emphasis is on what Jesus has done and is now doing for us while seated at the right side of God, not on your limits and failures. After making one sacrifice for sins forever, this man sat down at God's right hand. The scripture says in Hebrews 10:14, "For by one offering he hath perfected forever them that are sanctified." The secret of abundant life is to have a righteousness consciousness and not a sin consciousness. The truth is, "If we say that we have no sin, we deceive ourselves, and the truth is not in us, [but] If we confess our sins, He is faithful and just to forgive us *our* sins and to cleanse us from all unrighteousness." [1 John 1:9]

> "that is, that God was in Christ reconciling the world to Himself, not imputing their trespasses to them, and has committed to us the word of reconciliation. Now then, we are ambassadors for Christ, as though God were pleading through us: we implore *you* on Christ's behalf, be reconciled to God."
> — 2 CORINTHIANS 5:19-20

My friends, Righteousness consciousness sets you free from bondage to enjoy God's blessing and favor. For sin shall not have dominion over you, for you are not under the law but under grace. [Romans 6:14]. Our sinful nature perished, and a righteous nature was born in us when we made Jesus the Lord of our lives.

However, the scripture says in 1 John 2:1, "If any man sin, we have an advocate with the Father, Jesus Christ the righteous." God dealt with the problem, when Jesus became sin for us on the cross and banished sin, God took care of the issue. Thanks be to God; you can walk in the blessing and favour of God because you have a righteous nature and not a sinful nature.

NO LONGER SLAVES OF SIN

"For sin shall not have dominion over you, for you are not under law but under grace. What then? Shall we sin because we are not under law but under grace? Certainly not. Do you not know that to whom you present yourselves slaves to obey, you are that one's slaves whom you obey, whether of sin *leading* to death, or of obedience *leading* to righteousness? But God be thanked that *though* you were slaves of sin, yet you obeyed from the heart that form of doctrine to which you were delivered. And having been set free from sin, you became slaves of righteousness."

— ROMANS 6:14-18

Righteousness consciousness is always looking unto Jesus the author and finisher of our faith. [Hebrew 12:2]. That is the place of spiritual power and your authority as a believer over the forces of darkness. Unless you give Satan power over you, he has no control over you. Jesus has taken away all his power and given it to you. The scripture says, in Luke 10:18-20 "And he said unto them, I beheld Satan as lightning fall from heaven. Behold, I give unto you the power to tread on serpents and scorpions, and over all the power of the enemy: and nothing shall by any means hurt you. Notwithstanding in this rejoice not, that the spirits are subject unto you; but rather rejoice, because your names are written in heaven."

The secret to receiving blessings is to be established in the consciousness of your righteousness because the devil will bring lies and deceptions to your mind. As a believer, you are fighting against the forces of evil, and the only way you can win is by the might of God. For Christians to lead a successful life, they must be strong in the Lord and the might of His majesty. It is being in Christ that gives the believers their power. Without Him, we are powerless, but in Christ, we have access to all His favor, blessing, liberty, and power by putting our complete faith in the Lord's might. Realizing our complete dependence on God gives us true Christian authority.

Some Christians place their confidence in self-righteousness and wonder why they have wavering faith, filled with insecurity and fear. We are invited to be rooted in Christ. Colossians 2:6-7, "As you, therefore, have received Christ Jesus the Lord, so walk in Him, rooted and built up in Him and established in the faith, as you have been taught, abounding in it with thanksgiving." The forces of darkness will fight you to destroy your understanding of righteousness consciousness for you to start assuming that you simply have to be self-righteous by doing what is right to attain righteousness. God wants you in control of your situation. You were made in God's image, and you function like God. What sets you apart is your understanding of your righteousness.

Righteousness consciousness is the right image of the believer and the target of the devil's attacks to take advantage of you and your blessings. The Devil wants you to take your eyes off Jesus Christ's righteousness, the Word, and the Holy Spirit and to be controlled by your circumstances and mind. God shows immeasurable grace to the righteous, and God's grace brings enormous blessings in terms of peace and joy. When you feel God's grace, God's fullness of joy appears in your life. This visible evidence always shows that you have God's approval. Righteousness consciousness is always looking unto Jesus the author and finisher of our faith and that is the place of blessings, favor, and rest.

NINE

Righteous Joyful And Peaceful Life

DISCIPLINE YOURSELF TO LET THE WORD OF GOD direct your life and regenerate your mind. Let the word of Christ dwell in you richly, teaching and admonishing one another in all wisdom, singing psalms and hymns and spiritual songs, with thankfulness in your hearts to God. [Colossians 3:16].

Take your eyes off your self-righteousness and use your faith every day to believe that you are indeed righteous in Christ and that this righteousness is of the Lord's doing, not your own doing. The kingdom of God is revealed in "righteousness and peace and joy in the Holy Spirit." [Romans 14:17]. The Lord has given every believer His peace which is anxiety-free living. The believer receiving the gift of righteousness is complete in Christ because it refers to aligning one's nature with God's Holy plan and purpose.

> "For the kingdom of God is not eating and drinking, but righteousness and peace and joy in the Holy Spirit. For he who serves Christ in these things *is* acceptable to God and approved by men. Therefore, let us pursue the

things *which make* for peace and the things by which one may edify another."

— ROMANS 14:17-19

The scripture in Romans 8:28, says "And we know that all things work together for good to them that love God, to them who are the called according to *his* purpose." Every believer, under God's providence, can rejoice because all things, even their challenges, trials, and persecutions, are working together for the blessing. The law of the Spirit of life has set you free. [Romans 8:2]. You have the freedom to choose to be a slave to sin which leads to death (or the law of sin and death) or you can be a slave to obedience which leads to righteousness (or the law of the Spirit of life). The right choice is to be a slave to obedience which leads to righteousness consciousness.

They have this priceless reassurance that they are called according to God's purpose and love. We rejoice when we recognize God's goodness in our lives. My friends, we can be assured that there is nothing we need that God has not or will not provide for us. We must purpose in our heart to make use of what God has given us

"For the law of the Spirit of life has set you free in Christ Jesus from the law of sin and death."

— ROMANS 8:2

Righteousness Consciousness is always rejoicing in the Lord, for only in Jesus can we always experience a fullness of joy that is an overflowing and jubilant delight in the heart. This comes from believing God, because Sin consciousness is the result of believing a lie i.e., Satan – the father of liars. God accepts us because of Christ's righteousness. The pathway of life is to conform our nature with God's Holy standard by His grace and the power of the Holy Spirit that lives in us.

"For sin shall not have dominion over you, for you are not under law but under grace."

— ROMANS 6:14

There is fullness of joy in righteous living because God "justifies the ungodly" through faith. [Romans 4:5] Justification is the Christian doctrine that deals with God's acceptance of us into the right relationship with Him. To be justified implies that the righteous Judge declares us righteous.

> "Rejoice always, pray without ceasing, in everything give thanks; for this is the will of God in Christ Jesus for you."
> ## — 1 THESSALONIANS 5:16-18

Rejoice! Jesus is our righteousness, because we have been declared righteous, and fully accepted by God, not because of any righteousness in us, but only through faith. We have joy as we look outside ourselves and praise God for joining us in His righteousness. We should purposely choose to walk in God's righteousness with determination. For in Him we live and move and have our being, as also some of your own poets have said, 'For we are also His offspring. [Acts 17:28].

Therefore, since we are the offspring of God, we ought not to think that the Divine Nature is like gold or silver or stone, something shaped by art and man's devising. Truly, these times of ignorance God overlooked, but now commands all men everywhere to repent, because He has appointed a day on which He will judge the world in righteousness by the Man whom He has ordained. He has given assurance of this to all by raising Him from the dead." [Acts 17:29-30]. Righteousness Consciousness is a life of walking with God by faith because God is just and holy, and we have promises of peace and joy. A righteous lifestyle is full of joy, peace, and trust in the guidance of the Holy Spirit.

The Holy Spirit that dwells in every believer is the key to a righteous life. Those who trust God are strong in Him and in the power of His might in every circumstance because God wants all His children to grow to maturity in Christ. [Romans 8:14-16]. Attempting to live by our righteousness is always the source of this immaturity in Christ. That is living under the law instead of living under grace. This is an arena full of condemnation and there is no life in this kind of ministry.

The law is holy, but because it is impossible to perfectly keep the law, it gives everyone who lives by it, a constant sense of inadequacy or failure. Living the Christian life by the law and trying to keep all the rules and regulations will only lead to continuous frustration and is full of disappointment. Being under the law is a ritual or legal self-imposed bondage because it steals our joy.

People who are under a religious or legal mindset are those who use a code of obedience as a rule of duty, to meet moral requirements, salvation, sanctification, or righteousness; to become holy, remain holy, or gain approval from God. By sending Jesus to fulfill the law on our behalf, the Lord has set us free and whom the Son has set free is free indeed. God has not only freed us from the guilt of sin but has given us the power to live in righteousness.

Righteousness consciousness gives us access to the throne room of God which is full of joy. We are encouraged throughout the scriptures to remain faithful and obedient to God so that we would inherit the "crown of life" and wear the "raiment of righteousness." We are not children of darkness but of light, having fellowship with those who walk in the light because God is Light and imitating Him as humble children.

We don't have to be perfect to do God's will or imitate Him. We need to model ourselves after God's way of being and submit ourselves to righteousness. The power to submit to God's righteousness is a gift from God that is a consequence of the salvation granted to us through the death and resurrection of Jesus Christ.

Righteousness is granted to us through Christ's obedience, and we maintain our joy of righteousness through continuous obedience. We must with humility take heed, and never take for granted the grace of God. To be under grace means to be under the power of the Holy Spirit to live in the obedience that comes from faith and to serve others in love. A righteous lifestyle is also growth in godliness and holiness.

The outcome purpose is a life full of praise and joy which further creates a connection between you and the Lord. Every human being is a work in progress because we are saved by grace, justified, declared righteous, and delivered from a life of injustice by God with the righteousness of Christ. We are then sanctified so that our ways, thoughts, words, and deeds may reflect God's Righteousness in practice.

> "Listen to Me, you who know righteousness, You people in whose heart is My law: Do not fear the reproach of men, Nor be afraid of their insults."
> — ISAIAH **51:7**

The scriptures say in Romans 5:19 "For as by one man's disobedience many were made sinners, so by the obedience of one shall many be made righteous." Forgiveness of sins or justification is a gift not based on our obedience but rather on the obedience of one man, Jesus Christ: The scriptures say in 2 Cor 5:21 that God has given you the gift of righteousness. "For He (God) made Him (Jesus) who knew no sin to be sin for us, that we might become the righteousness of God in Him." When you accepted Jesus as your Lord, He gave to you the wonderful gift of His righteousness.

Righteousness consciousness leads to a righteous lifestyle. Endeavor to always present your body as servants to righteousness which leads to holiness and sanctification. We should obey righteousness instead of our sinful desires. We boast in God through our Lord Jesus Christ, through whom we have now received reconciliation, but we must strive for holiness without which we will not see God. Thus, obedience comes from faith, and such genuine faith results in genuine works.

Finally, righteousness consciousness is having a right relationship with God. The harvest of righteousness is sown in peace by those who make peace. [James 3:18]. That is peace with God and mankind. My friend be filled with the fruit of righteousness that comes through Jesus Christ, to the glory and praise of God. Therefore, having been made righteous by faith, we have peace with God through our Lord Jesus Christ. [Romans 5:1]. The fruit of righteousness will be peace; the effect of righteousness will be peace and trust forever.

> "Through Him, we have received grace and apostleship for obedience to the faith among all nations for His name"
>
> — ROMANS1:5

Confession Section

7 DAYS TO DECLARE YOUR RIGHTEOUSNESS

1. Father, I declare no weapon formed against me will prosper because I have the righteousness of Jesus Christ.

2. I declare that every tongue that rises up against me in judgment and condemnation. I have the right to condemn because I am righteous in Christ.

3. I declare that I have the Father's gift of righteousness; I will reign in life through Christ.

4. I declare that Abraham's blessings are mine, "Christ has redeemed us from the curse of the law, having become a curse for us (for it is written, cursed *is* everyone who hangs on a tree"), that the blessing of Abraham might come upon the Gentiles in Christ Jesus, that we might receive the promise of the Spirit through faith. [Galatians 3:13-14]

5. I declare that I live by faith "For I am not ashamed of the gospel of Christ, for it is the power of God to salvation to everyone who believes, to the Jew first and also to the Greek. For in it the righteousness of God is revealed from faith to faith; as it is written, the just shall live by faith." [Romans 1:16-17]

6. I declare that I am Filled with the fruit of righteousness that comes through Jesus Christ, to the glory and praise of God.

7. I declare that He who supplies seed to the Sower and bread for food will supply and multiply my seed for sowing and increase the harvest of His righteousness.

Thank You!

I'd like to use this time to thank you for purchasing my books and helping my ministry

You have already accomplished so much, but I would appreciate an honest review of some of my books on your favorite retailer. This is critical since reviews reflect how much an author's work is respected.

Please be aware that I read and value all comments and reviews. You can always post a review even though you haven't finished the book yet and then edit your reviews later.

Thank you so much as you spare a precious moment of your time and may God bless you and meet you at the very point of your need.

Please send me an email at <u>dr.pastormanny@gmail.com</u> if you encounter any difficulty in leaving your review.

You can also send me an email at <u>dr.pastormanny@gmail.com</u>

If you need prayers or counsel or if you have questions. Better still if you want to be friends with me.

OTHER BOOKS BY EMMANUEL ATOE

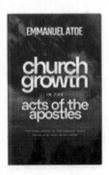

Church Growth in the Acts of the Apostles

The Church is the most powerful corporate body that is capable of commanding the attention of heaven on earth. The Church is God's idea and product, and so possesses an inbuilt capacity for success. The objective of this book is to get you acquainted with the purpose of the church in general, and the vision of Victory Sanctuary in particular.

A Moment of Prayer

There is nothing impossible with God but praying while breaking the law of God makes your prayers ineffective. Therefore, in this book, A Moment of Prayer, everyone under this program is expected to pray according to the rule, not against the law supporting it.

The Believer's Handbook

This book is highly recommendable for all. It is a book that will enhance your spiritual life, ignite the fire in you. It is a book that will open you heart to the mystery of faith.

The inestimable value of this book to every soul cannot be over emphasized. With this book you will get to know about the pillars of true faith in God. If you have been doubting your salvation, Christian life, the person and baptism of the Holy Ghost etc., this book is all you need.

OTHER BOOKS BY EMMANUEL ATOE

Wisdom for your Best Life

God's wisdom is an essential tool in the journey of every believer. The Bible contrasts wisdom from above, which seeks to please God and is fulfilling, from earthly wisdom, which is self-seeking and leads to ruin. The indispensability of wisdom is underscored by the biblical saying, "Wisdom is the principal thing" and "In all your getting, get wisdom."

The First Five Ps that changed my Life

The first five Ps that Changed My Life hopefully will change your life for good and for the best. Living your best life in five Ps is possible. Dr. Emmanuel O. Atoe wrote this life experiences book that is so powerful that it will change your story for good. If the principles explained in this book is applied correctly, you will achieve the desire of your heart.

Printed in the United States
by Baker & Taylor Publisher Services